Wired For Genius

Memoirs of a Social Oddity

J. Matthew Jacobson

 Mithras Returning Publishing

ISBN: 978-8-663-70113-6

Library of Congress Control Number: 2020XXXXXX

Printed in the United States of America.

First printing edition 2020.

Artwork and design by Thanks Universe! Arts

Mithras Returning Publishing House

1611 Cottonwood Dr Ste. 9

Louisville, CO, 80027

Special thank you to Dr. Tony Attwood, Dr. Simon Baron-Cohen, and Psy.D. Christian Stewart-Ferrer for all their hard work and sacrifice to bring awareness to all of us.

Sincerely,

We, the lost generation of autism.

Dedicated to

Heather Redfern

Your unconditional friendship and nonjudgmental companionship are the rarest of treasures.

Contents

Introduction

I never thought I was exceptional at anything. I'm barely coordinated enough to navigate daily life; God forbid I should willingly add the variable of sports to my normally occurring obstacles. I have a list of problems that are odd and unresolved. One of the most annoying of which is something I call chronological memory. Years, dates, and times rarely ever serve as anchoring points for my memory. If memory serves, I graduated from high school in the bottom 20 percent of my class. I never thought I was dumb. I am completely guilty of failing to find the appeal in learning the materials that were preselected and prescribed for me since I was a child.

When it was time to take the SAT in high school, I played the random pattern game. I just filled in the dots semi-haphazardly, but would gravitate towards B or C. I think I scored around the 770 range. A quick internet search lands that score in the bottom 7-14% category. I didn't care. In all of my infinite wisdom I was never going to a college or university. I never wanted to. I never wanted to be in a singular profession. In fact, the only test I ever took seriously was the ASVAB, and that was only because anything less than an exceptional score meant a possibility (in the event of a draft) that would narrow my options to digging a ditch with a rifle slung across my back or running towards open fire. Neither of which sounded like much fun.

Ironically, I would end up serving 8 years in the United States Air Force and attending two colleges and two universities. My whole life is a series of ironic events. I was originally enlisted to become a loadmaster. I did fairly well in technical school until I had a timed test that included what I would call "extra-long division" and had only a pencil and piece of paper to complete the test. I never was very good at math. That led to me being reclassified into another job. I will never forget being on the phone with my mom awaiting my new job classification, the one I didn't get to pick. I told her I really didn't care what my job was, as long as it wasn't working with bombs. On the day I went to retrieve my new job field, the paperwork said Munitions Systems.

That would be my job field for the next 7+ years. Munitions Systems, or AMMO for short was a pretty cool job. We had security clearances, learned all about bombs, missiles, aircraft flares, various portable explosives, drank copious amounts of beer, and generally promoted Esprit de Corps and blowing stuff up. I was no absolutely perfect Airman, but I did manage to get out with an Honorable Discharge, a ton of great friends, and the experience of protecting a base in England directly after 9/11 and helping to launch and execute the Shock and Awe Air Campaign.

I have never wanted conflict. I was never a fighter. I was big enough in stature and courteous enough in nature to never engulf myself in those situations. Most of this world has never made any sense to me. I have never felt in unison with the dominant thought patterns of "normal" humanity. This has apparently become known as Other World Syndrome. Essentially, it is the sense that you truly feel like you are from another planet. This feeling is constructed and reinforced by the observation and analyzation of others, followed by an introspective awareness of your personal difference when compared to other individual and societal differences.

It is my sincere hope and desire that this simple book may serve to help understand the thoughts and actions of those that relate to my own experiences. This might even include yourself!

It All Began

It may initially seem like an awkward place to begin, but anything normal just wouldn't be par for my life. Hence my story beginning at age forty-three. Two years into my university educational pursuit, I am yet again finding it incredibly hard to find the motivation to focus on my classes. I absolutely crave learning. My greatest hinderance is finding interest in the various subjects I was studying. Once back inside the four walls of my apartment, my curiosity defaults to the random subjects that cross my mind. At the moment, it was thinking back to a paper I had written a few years back while living in Amarillo.

In my then boredom of waiting to start at Amarillo College, I had written a paper titled The Spherical Nature of the Universe and the Laws that Govern It. Without diving into the details, I was curious as to how I could update the paper to more accurately include the dynamics of the plasmid electric universe theory. As I began refreshing myself with the paper I wrote, I was unsatisfied with the very basic level of electricity that I knew. I had never worked as an electrician. I was always fine at problem solving mechanical or electrical failures, but the depth of knowledge in how electricity works at the electron level was lacking.

I began watching some basic videos on electrons, protons, and neutrons. I was essentially learning from scratch. I have always had a rare gift of seeing patterns. It doesn't take much try, if any. If I have learned anything, it is that most things will carry an underlying pattern. The only obstacle is to find it. It's incredibly easy (for me) visually and relatively easy audibly to uncover patterns. That being said, my brain continually asks, "Where or what is the pattern?" in every subject, situation, and scenario.

Educating myself on electrons and the electron orbitals led me to referencing those parameters that would coincide with the Periodic Table. Finding the link between elemental rows and orbitals, I searched online to find what the orbital arrangement of some predicted elements would be, according to the various sources. When I noticed an incredibly famous open-source site had an orbital arrangement for Element 122 that appeared to be wrong (to my mind), an all too common switch flipped in my head.

From that moment on, I obsessed on proving my assumption. In order to affirm my assumptions, I spent countless hours that turned into days writing out the electron orbitals in a manner my mind could best visualize. I knew the pattern that governs the orbitals and was able to write them all out to the extent of what would be referred to as Predicted Element 300. Keep in mind, Element 118 is the last element man has successfully been able to create.

All of this was done with a hyper-focus that blocked out nearly every aspect of daily life. For sake of purity in disclosure, this "triggered" hyper-focus neglected showering, eating, brushing of teeth, and university class attendance. I'm not proud of this aspect. I am hardly conscious of it when it is flipped on and I'm certainly unable to quash my researching. Even if I pass out, I will return directly to researching and working to resolve the issue. There is no priority above that of resolving the issue and acquiring a final answer or solution.

Eventually, I had reached the conclusion and successfully proved that the electron orbital configuration I had read on the internet was in fact inaccurate. It was an obsession that lasted at least a day and a half. I went from barely knowing more than protons are positive and electrons are negative, to pointing out inaccuracies in the electron orbital configuration of an element that hasn't even been created. That's the up side of my mind. The down side is that when I laid down to finally go to sleep, I had spent so much brainpower obsessing towards a resolution that I had a complete emotional breakdown. I never cry, but that night I cried and broke down to a total mess. This is a real situation that some people might not be able to conceive, but I was so mentally exhausted that when I had a fleeting thought to retrieve my own age from memory, I couldn't. I had to google my full birthdate to see how old I was. I actually couldn't remember, and couldn't do the simplest of subtraction to find out.

The Awakening

After extensive and exhaustive research in the field of electrons, and after emotionally breaking down the night I finally reached a conclusion, I passed out. The next morning, I woke up well-refreshed and a bit reflective on the previous day(s) obsession. My default mode then is to learn about things that cross my mind that I have interest in.

I began watching various videos on child prodigies. Watching several of those videos led to the topic of the mind and of brain function. My autistic "Ah Ha!" moment occurred when I clicked on a two-and-a-half-minute video clip the Smithsonian Channel®

released titled, "Did Asperger's Syndrome Contribute to Newton's Genius?". It was suggested by the platform's algorithms, and I love learning about the greats of science past. I have read Tesla's writings, Benjamin Franklin's Autobiography, and several books on Einstein and his works. I didn't know what Asperger's Syndrome was. I had never researched the topic. I have a friend or two with children that are on the proverbial spectrum, but nothing else to relate to. You wouldn't think that such a short video would contribute to the self-diagnosis of autism or that it would be the catalyst that eventually provided the most solid understanding of myself that I have ever held, but it did!

Imagine living the last previous days as I have described in the previous chapter. Imagine having the quiet awareness of emphatically researching a topic minus the ability to truly rest until concrete resolution occurs. Now, imagine a calmer mind casually watching videos. A mind just one day later that is fully mentally and emotionally recovered. Suddenly, this video abruptly begins and various gentlemen begin describing Isaac Newton as; working obsessively, reclusive, constantly writing material that no one else reads and isn't for anyone else in particular, having an enormous capacity to hyper-focus, asking fundamental questions, having a persistence to question until finding a solution, seemingly conditional keys of his characteristics were traits like poor social relationships, poor empathy, problems reading faces, reading body language, auto-repetitive behaviors, extremely narrow interests, complete subject obsession, pushing one's self to the limit during distracted behaviors, and capable of complete tunnel-vision with whatever he was doing. The video continues to note that the Asperger's brain works more like having multiple computers in the brain operating independently and unlinked as opposed to the normal and typical brain. It explained this as a term referred to as "local processing" that operates far superior to the typical "integrated" brain. A simple Google® search of Autistic Brain Wired Differently produces over 1.5 million results.

Anyway, had I watched this video with more time elapsing than one night after experiencing my own episode, I probably would have simply been envious of those great men of history. That was not to be the case. Sure, this two minute and thirty-three second video isn't and should never serve as a diagnosis and every human inherently shares many various characteristics. This was different, though. This was logic. This was The Universe telling me to, "Look here, son. I've got something for ya." And sure enough, it did.

I spend the next few days learning everything I could about Autism and Asperger's Syndrome. I watched countless lectures on the subject. I read Tony Attwood's 'The Complete Guide to Asperger's Syndrome'. I read the DSM's different changes in definition and classification. I consumed articles, TED®

Talks, and multiple YouTube® videos by a population of people that joyously referred to themselves as Aspies. On a personal note, I dislike the term Aspie, but I do feel that using the term Asperger's or High Functioning Autism better conveys the dynamics of my life experiences, thought process, and various social oddness. Autism as an identifier, seems to conjure up visions of Dustin Hoffman's Rain Man character or other constructs that separate the individual from the reality that a spectrum has countless variations per characteristic. I learned there is even an entire generation of middle-aged adults that evaded diagnosis for various reasons.

At every step of information consumption, I was continually pinged with reading or listening to attributes that caused a flood of realizations from past things that directly mirrored what I was learning. It was the equivalent to listening to stranger describe your very life and nature.

I am not sure if 'symptom' is the appropriate word, but the physical and mental traits that I was reading and hearing about led to the construction of a framework existing on the autism spectrum. This framework was becoming so incredibly solid that I could not dispute it. In the following chapters, I will address those traits and how they have resonated through my life experiences.

Patterns in Everything

I have always had a proficiency in pattern recognition. It typically isn't anything that requires work. Most of the time, it seems to be something that actually jumps out to me with no effort at all. Many years ago, I saw a very talented musician (though more regionally known) post a picture of his new tattoo to his Facebook® page. The tattoo was a creatively constructed design. He got the phrase "An eye for an eye makes the whole world blind" inked on his forearm. Instead of using typical letters, he used braille dots distinguished by having two different sized dots (large vs, small) arranged in a grouping as to represent the letter equivalent. Immediately upon seeing the picture he posted, my internal thought response was, "Man, they messed that up.". I don't know any blind people. I have never studied the various braille symbols. I only know what it said because he stated it. How was I able to immediately see the "typo" in his fresh new ink? To me it was simple. I read the tattoo as it was explained. The letter E occurs seven times in that Gandhi quote. Twice it occurs perfectly spaced before and after the letter Y. That alone was plenty enough information to solidify what constitutes the letter E. Unfortunately, the tattoo artist used a large sized in dot on the 4th occurrence of the letter E instead of using the smaller dot. The second conundrum was that in order to be able to correct the tattoo, you would have to make every single large dot the new small dots, and then go back over the whole piece and make even larger dots where large dots are now required. That's a long explanation, and I'm sure most people if tasked, could eventually go through and find the wrong dot. My brain did the cumulation of all of those steps in merely a second.

When I was going through the admission process at Amarillo College, they informed me of needing to take a Texas placement exam. Initially, I was a little more than worried about how well I would do as a middle-aged male attending school with a predominant population of 18 and 20-year-olds fresh out of high school. Eventually, I didn't mind. It had been 10 years since I had attempted any further education, but I was optimistic. Part of my optimism came from the results of a full-scale WAIS intellectual assessment (I.Q test) that was administered by a phenomenal Veteran's Administration Psychologist, Dr. Paul Whittaker. I remember the frustration of missing a couple of answers on one of the sublets, or subtests. Dr

Whittaker looked at me almost whimsically. He said, "You know you're not going to get *all* of them right, *right*?". Although I could get the humor in his response to my self-inflicted frustration, I was on a mission. I had something to prove, albeit primarily to myself. This was coming from the guy who struggled with everything, graduated in the lower quarter of my high school class, no SAT score to speak of, and about to attend college as I am cresting the infamous hill of turning 40. Fortunately, even at what I am pretty sure is the greatest age-based deduction range of all, I was able to test out with a score comfortably north of the MENSA® acceptance range. My very highest scores were from the subtests of Similarities, Comprehension, and Matrix Reasoning. Those areas all whisper, "autism". I would later learn through association that MENSA® is often known as a hub for people with Autism Spectrum Disorder (ASD). It isn't an I.Q. score-based ego that unites us, as much as it is the social quirkiness.

With this newfound confidence, I later spent an afternoon taking the placement exams for college. My vocabulary and other writing-type skills tested far above the normal and even above normal range.

My mathematics results however, were so atrocious that I was required to take TWO remedial courses! How embarrassing! It would prove to have a great impact on this whole adventure I call life, though. I was blessed to have the most perfect instructor for these remedial classes. Mrs. Edie Carter, Dean of Academic Success/Department Chair and Professor of Developmental Mathematics, opened her class with a statement that changed my outlook of math in general. She told the class that everyone who was in remedial math was there likely because they either had life events that were distractions to learning, or that they didn't like their teacher or vice versa. For me, it was my high school teacher's piercing voice and typically short attitude made focusing an impossibility.

Professor Carter was the first person to truly understand the way my mind works. She had two sons that went to Harvard, and one of them seemed similar to myself in processing styles. I think she could also tell, because I would ask questions that made the class scratch their heads, but she always knew exactly what I was asking.

I once asked Prof. Carter how she knew what number(s) came next in the list of perfect squares. She said that when she was going through classes, they were simply told to memorize them. I asked her about the pattern and she said that perhaps I'll be the one to figure it out. I went home that afternoon and chartered them until the pattern was clear. The next day of class, I arrived early to show her how the numbers move through a series of 0, 1, 4, 9, 6, 5 and then back down to 6, 9, 4, 1, to 0 in an eternal cycle. I let her read my paper on The Spherical Nature of the Universe, to which she gave me my favorite one-word compliment ever, "Brilliant!". She even knew that I had problems showing my work, but not with solving the problem (I would skip unnecessary or redundant steps in my head) and she would always show tolerance and understanding around that. I am not surprised that she was the recipient of the American Association of Community Colleges 2017 Faculty Innovation Award.

While living in Missouri, I would often sit on a friend's porch and simply observe the surroundings. I began counting and studying the branching of walnut trees. I found they at first glance may look even, but were twice as likely to branch in one direction than the opposite. I forget the specific compass quarter direction that the branches dominated, but it was very obvious. In trying to find the usefulness in knowing the ratio of directional branch growth, I realized that the gathering of walnuts could be optimized if groves were planted in alignment with the branch growth.

This ability to rapidly recognize patterns has always been my favorite "superpower". Its usefulness has manifested in various ways and wasn't self-realized until later in life. I remember as a kid, I would enjoy competing in word search contests against the other kids in our church youth group, and would often win. I don't know if that is relevant or not. What I do know, is that if you happen to be a pattern-based thinker, congratulations! You certainly have a peculiar advantage above the neurotypical thought processes.

The Great Flood

Once I began learning the various traits of this strange new Asperger's thing, I experienced a rush of memories that correlated to what I was reading and listening to. There are several things that a variety of people can easily relate to, I understand that. Some things that neurotypical people experience are exponentially intensified in those on the autism spectrum. Sometimes those traits are not so intense or they are incredibly specific in annoyance.

One of the conditions most recognizable in myself is one that I truly believed was unique to just to me. I had no clue or reason to assume anyone else even mildly related. This condition has affected me on a predominantly social stage. It is referred to as Auditory Processing Disorder.

Auditory Processing Disorder (APD) occurs when audible information (for various reasons) is essentially ill-received or hyper-received. In my own experience, this manifests predominantly as an inability to focus on one particular stream of information, such as a person speaking to me, due to the abundance of other separate streams or sources of sound being processed at the seemingly the same level with that which I am trying to focus on. One example is an inability to focus in the classroom. I can focus intensely on the teacher or professor's message and be tormented mentally by the concurrent influx of other noises that most would consider nominal. I hear the tapping of a pencil, the squeak of a desk, the wind against the window, the cough or clearing of the throat in one student, the huff or hum response of another student, and the drone of an air conditioning unit with near equivalency. Also, it is important to remember that even in the classroom I am continually deconstructing those noises that are being received equally. Why is person *X* tapping their pencil? Are they annoyed at the topic? Bored by the subject? What is the rhythm? Why is person *Y* huffing at the last comment the professor made? Is person *Z* sick? That's the third time in 2 minutes they have coughed.

This also becomes tortuous when in environments where multiple small-group socializing occurs. If I am to go to restaurant and sit at a table with a friend, it takes all of my energy to focus on the conversation at hand, because I can't filter out the information that I don't need. It is extremely difficult to decode, interpret, and even remember what the person directly in front of me is saying. I am equally processing the girl complaining about her boyfriend at table #1, the parent bragging about their child to a coworker at table #3, the ice in a metal tumbler being shaken by the bartender, and cheers or jeers of the sports fans glued to the game on the big screen.

I also have great issue with certain voices. This is a difficult thing to explain, but something I think may be more common throughout society. All I can tell you is that it seems to occur more frequently in female voices that are both higher pitched and a bit scratchy (like my high school math teacher). I am also an eternal critic and personally tend to be more monotone. Some of this is due to the constant analyzing of the person's delivery and intent. Why are they so sing-song in delivery? Why are they so heavily accentuating their points? You're trying too hard to sell me. Those are my internal thoughts conglomerated whist trying my best to be present and engaged with the person in front of me. That's my audible world, however odd or crazy.

I have always been that way; I just was far less conscious of it as a child. I was the second born of four kids in a two-parent household. Needless to say, there was a lot going on. In conversation with my mom 30+ years after the fact, I asked her to tell me the specifics of my hearing issues as a pre-teen. She told me flat out that I "couldn't hear". As a disclaimer, we grew up in a fairly strict household. We learned at an early age that our parents (as well as all adults) were to be spoken to with respect and that disrespect had a zero-tolerance policy.

"What do you mean I couldn't hear", I asked her. She then proceeded to tell me examples of how she would call and call me to come or ask me something and I was completely *seemingly* oblivious to what was going on. This became such an issue that I was suggested by a doctor to undergo the process of having tubes put in my ears. What her and the doctor could not figure out (remember, this is mid 1980's), was that when I went into the well-insulated hearing booth, given giant soft earphones, and tasked with pushing a red button upon hearing the sound, I did just fine. Thankfully, the option of having tubes put in eventually was discarded. I learned just this year that there is a growing belief that many of the kids of my generation that had tubes put in were very possibly simply suffering from APD. It is important to note that APD is not a physical ear component function issue, but a neurologically-linked processing disorder. As I was discussing the contents of this book with my younger sister, she informed me that she had similar hearing issues that resulted in her being tested and found to have APD.

On a side note, I am probably guilty of breaking some world record for the number of times and length of time I have listened to Canon in D Major on repeat. I highly recommend the Mainz Chamber Orchestra version conducted by Gunter Kehr. I never examined just how frequently I kept my earbuds in or only played one particular song on repeat, until this great flood occurred. I certainly understand now why all those weird autistic kids love their noise-cancelling earphones. I just was too oblivious to know that I was one!

"Look at me when I'm talking to you!", is a phrase I heard constantly from my Dad growing up. Eye contact can be a common trait occurring throughout the spectrum. It didn't take long for me to adjust my actions and mannerisms to his authority, and as a result, I now have far less issues with that. I understand people not wanting to do it, though. It adds an entire set of variables of distraction to your thought process. Unfortunately, on the opposite side of this matter, I have to keep a consciously timed measure of judgement in my head to make sure I don't over-stare. I have gotten comments about that from people. That will make you feel just as awkward, I promise.

Who Are You?

I find it easy to relate to the Absent-Minded Professor stigma. I have no chronological memory to speak of. I have never been able to look at a photograph and immediately remember the year or month in which it was taken, unless it was tied to something absolutely monumental such as a life event. I know what year I was born, the year I graduated high school, the year I entered the service, was discharged from service, and what year it is now as I am typing this. That's about it. Seriously.

My train of thought is linked to incorporate so many other possibly relative topical insertions that with any length of conversation, I guarantee you I will eventually (from 10 minutes to hours later) say, "Oh! My point about mentioning *X* was *Y*". That can get embarrassing. There is little more embarrassing than what I learned was another actual specific condition and not just my generic absent-mindedness. This is a condition called face-blindness or Prosopagnosia.

Face blindness is a condition where the face of a person you have previously met either doesn't get filed into your memory or so loosely gets filed, that extremely identical appearance (an often location) is necessary to identify the person. 60 Minutes® did a great special on face blindness that I would highly recommend if you are hearing about this for the first time.

Like every other attribute on this planet, face blindness can occur on a spectrum. The opposite end of this spectrum are people who can remember faces they saw once, ten years ago as they were standing at a checkout counter purchasing an item. I am not completely face blind, but it does take effort, it takes repetition, familiarity, and is often hinged on environment as an early memory anchor.

My neighbor had recently moved in about three doors down. The first time I met him, he was with a friend of his that was just visiting. I often don't remember people's names the first time I meet them. This became such a nuisance that I have since learned to ask someone multiple times in hopes of it sticking in my memory. When I met my neighbor, he introduced himself as what I thought was Peter and then he introduced me to his friend James. While we were talking trivialities, I thought, "great, Peter and James, just like in the Bible". That should be easy enough to remember. At some later point, Pete corrected me on calling him Peter. My bad. I can remember that. A couple of weeks later, Pete was coming up the stairs and he stopped to chat. A minute later, his friend walks up and we exchange cordial hey, what's ups. Me being the polite person I was raised to be, I stuck out my hand and said, "I'm Jeremy, btw." Embarrassingly, he politely responded, "We've met. I'm James." You don't know what to say or how to act in those scenarios. I just apologized and said I didn't recognize you. I don't know how that made me look, but it certainly was awkward on my side.

I go to a Buddhist-inspired university. It is also quite a small university with less than 1,000 undergraduate and graduate students combined. It is typical for the smaller-sized classrooms to arrange the desks in a circular fashion. There is a lot of interpersonal work that occurs in the classroom, as well. Many times, we will forgo the desks altogether and sit on cushions directly on the floor, Buddhist-style. This may sound odd for a university, but the school offers courses in yoga, meditation, and even raga singing.

In one class, I was sitting beside a girl when the teacher told us to break up into twos. I looked over and did the awkward half-talk/half-gesture for "Wanna partner up?". We turned to face each other for whatever the instructor had in store for us. Again, like the good southern gentleman I aspire to be, I stuck out my hand and properly introduced myself. She told me her name, which to date, I still can't remember. After a few seconds, I then looked at her more intently and then looked around the room (for more blonde females). I then built up the nerve to ask her, "Did I give you a ride back to the main campus after class last Friday?". "Yeah!", she said. [In this short ride from one campus to another, we had laughed intensely, talked about our various travels, and generally hit it off.] One week later, she was a total stranger. Fortunately, I had just learned about face blindness between then and the last time I saw her. I was able to minimize the awkwardness by explaining the face blindness to her.

In a different class, I was sitting next to a girl, when again, the professor told us to break into groups of two. We were doing a practice where you sit Indian style facing the other person. You look at the person and listen to the person without responding or even reacting. You're just supposed to sit there and listen. No head nodding, no eye reactions, etc. We sat for 45 minutes looking at each other and listening to each other. Afterwards we got to talking and had the commonality of being from the south, which was rare for the more "granola" northwestern populous you generally see at the school. Anyway, after class we went and sat on the couch in a lounge area and had a good 10 to 15-minute conversation. The next time we had class, we were at a larger university for an offsite. Because we had just had such a great conversation, I was looking for her so I could say hi. Our class sat gathered around at a wire mesh row of tables. Forty minutes into class, I looked at this unfamiliar female sitting four feet away. Her name tag was just barely exposing the last three letters of her name that allowed me to figure out it was the same person! She was unrecognizable. Why? Because she had glasses on. There again, I had to courteously catch her the next time we had class and let her know about the face blindness and how I didn't want her to think I was being rude by not saying hi.

Don't Think I Don't Care

Another quite unfortunate characteristic of being on the spectrum is a trait known as mind blindness. Mind blindness relates to the inability to perceive intent, point of view, and empathies of others. I'm no psychologist, and even psychologists have not mastered the understanding of mind blindness. I have read many definitions on mind blindness and they all seem to hover around the social and communicative impairments experienced in autistic people. This entire book is written from a personal experiential account.

This section will be no different. I think I am fairly capable of navigating the social scenes. I simply prefer not to. It requires extra energy, it often is uninteresting or not educational, and there is an eternal awkwardness that eventually arises.

A personal example of this was when I was visiting a friend after quite a long absence. This person lived 1,500 miles away. I had no established length of stay that we had agreed upon. I knew I couldn't be there forever, just a week or two. I continually invested in her and her family both physically in acts of service and monetarily during my stay. One day she came out and informed me that she thought I was there long enough and that I basically needed to go. I said, "That's fine. I can leave right now!" And I started to get up. I was not being sharp or just flouncing. I was grateful for the tenure and hospitality and was simply seeking to remedy the situation. She said," No. No. You don't have to leave this very moment!" To which I replied, "But I don't want to be anywhere I'm not wanted or to be a hinderance on anyone."

Months later when we were on the phone, I was telling her about all that I was learning in this mind blindness field. She responded, "Well it makes sense. Remember when you were over here and I told you I thought it was time [for you] to leave. I tried to drop all kinds of hints to you." To this day I am unaware of any hints. I will give her the benefit of the doubt, but whatever her clues were, they were far too subtle to distinguish as a hint.

Mind blindness (to me) is the total encapsulation of social awkwardness. People seem far more excited about things than I can care to be. There is absolutely no logic to be found in dancing. I hate the process of saying goodbye. It's not the anticipated separation that I am dwelling on. More so, it is the ever-unfamiliar protocol by which it is all supposed to take place. I always feel like I'm torn between saying goodbye to everyone individually, and just sneaking away quietly. Depending on how close we are or how far back we go, I really just prefer to quietly slip away. I also don't want to be rude, because people are funny like that and they find offense quicker than anything else in existence.

Mind blindness is sometimes confused for or seen as a lack of empathy. I have heard it explained with relation to autistic people having fewer mirror neurons than neurotypical people. That diminishes their ability to naturally mimic what the other person is physically manifesting during the experience. Unlike sociopaths and psychopaths, autistic individuals actually do feel the joys and pains of others, they just don't know how to reflect back to the person that they do share the moment. The problem comes from knowing the best practices and protocols for physically or verbally expressing it, because it can seem like an unnatural reaction.

The most compassionate, non-judgmental, loving, and kindhearted person on this planet happens to be someone who accepts me wholly flawed, quirks and all. This dear companion has a history of depression and has battled with suicide. One day we were riding down the road to a concert and she told me how she had just come really close to committing suicide a few days earlier. I was driving, as she told me that. And I just stayed silent. And remained silent for a while.

A year later we were talking and I told her about the whole Theory of Mind, face blindness, and apparent (however inaccurate) lack of empathy. I was explaining the mirror neuron deficiency among other things. She was following along quite well, as she is a psychological reservoir of knowledge and a pupil of the greats like Carl Jung. She is absolutely without a doubt, the most intelligent woman I have ever met. Her level of humor reflects that. She's as beautiful as she is compassionate. Imagine how I felt hearing her tell me that when she mentioned to me in the car about how suicidal she was just days earlier and I didn't say anything, she "thought I didn't care." The woman [the only source of joy outside of my family 5 states away] that has been the most steadfast friend I have ever had... just told me she didn't think I cared if she lived or died. It's heart-wrenching. She's one of the elite handful out of 7,794,553,117 people on this planet that I absolutely want to ensure stays alive.

I heard what she said when we were in the car, I just didn't know what to say. What do you say? What do you do? Is she done telling me all she has to say? Should I just be there in the moment? How can I even help? I can't hug her. I'm driving down the road to a place I have never been on an unfamiliar route. She lives 30 miles away. I couldn't stop her if I tried. My heart hurts to hear this. I wish she saw herself the way I see her. Those are all of the things going through my head in this awkward moment. We have the kind of relationship where she can be that open. It's not the first time she has confided in me about similar moments. I've learned a lot in the last 4 decades. I still don't know what to with all the various situations.

I'm not prone to cry at funerals. My mind is thinking of everything present. When Grandmother (my mother's mom) died, I came to sit by her side in her home. I know she's no longer there. You know what I did? I did MATH. That's right. I calculated the length of time by which my Granddaddy and her were separated. He died in December of 1975 and she lived into the 21st Century. So, I did math for the amount of time by which the two had been separated and were now finally reunited. She loved him dearly and never remarried.

When Grandpa (my father's dad) died, it took deep observation of her crying in loneliness and mindful contemplation on the 50+ years they spent together physically on this earth and all that they built before I got emotional.

Between the *Who?* of face blindness and the *What?* of mind blindness, it's a miracle I manage anything.

If You Look Closely

As explained earlier, the more I learned from reading and hearing multiple PhDs describe Asperger's, the more I was forced to look at my own life without excuse. I learned that there are unique quirks and mannerisms that seem minutely odd in passing, but upon closer observation, they are pointing towards the spectrum of autism. No one single descriptor will be some kind of 'proof', but you simply can't be naturally inclined to recognize patterns and dismiss obvious signs.

One of the most dominant sensitivities witnessed by people with ASD is sensitivity to skin irritants such as certain fabrics. I was surprised to learn that t-shirt tags are one of the biggest irritants. My mind suddenly jumped back to the days of my youth. As soon as I was old enough to operate a pair of scissors, I was cutting the tags off of my shirts. Before that, I was ripping them out of my shirts, sometimes leaving an equally annoying hole in the back. Another bitter scoop of irony was learning that autistic individuals tend to wear placid and neutrally colored (typically black) t-shirts. These things sound simple, almost trivial to those on the outside looking in. I was faced with the realization that I have a closet full of black and gray tagless t-shirts. My laundry routine however, revolves around making sure I have one of my three identical loose-fitting black t-shirts to wear. I have tried to buy more, but the manufacturer has changed the dynamic of the shirts. They don't feel or fit the same as those three I bought a couple of years ago.

Another telltale sign of someone that may be autistic is in their shoes, or lack thereof. For example, I despise shoes. I don't mind wearing leather flipflops or sandals. Even in the coldest of weather, if I step outside to smoke a cigarette, I will only ever put on my sandals. I've had so many people comment to me on how my feet must be frozen. An odd few have even thought I was just trying to "act tough". That is ridiculous, but plays into the conglomerate of symptoms.

I learned about a sense called thermoception. This is our ability to sense temperature. Suffer is not the right word to use in this circumstance, but I certainly experience hyposensitivity to the cold. I will wear my trusty flipflops throughout the year. This appears extremely odd to anyone that has witnessed me in the grocery store while snow is accumulating outside on the ground. That becomes obvious by the crazy looks I get.

A couple of years ago I began learning and practicing sun gazing. Sun gazing is the practice of standing barefoot on natural soil, sand, or rock while focusing on the rising or setting sun. No, you aren't going to burn your eyes out, if you do it right. The UV ray levels experienced during the first and last 45-60 minutes of sunrise and sunset is 0 due to the curvature of the earth. I would never recommend doing it during the breadth of normal daylight, and most mobile weather sites on the internet can help verify the UV index based on location. With that said, I would often stand outside in the snow, barefoot and wearing shorts and a t-shirt, for up to 45 minutes at a time. If you really want to look like a weirdo, standing dead-still while being barefoot wearing summer clothes and standing in the snow as you're staring at the sun is one of the very best ways. I believe it was psychologist Christian

Stewart-Ferrer, University of Southern Denmark, that once said that the easiest way to spot someone with Asperger's Syndrome is to find the person in the group of friends that doesn't wear a jacket or coat in the winter.

Another shocking insight occurred when listening to Stewart-Ferrer's lecture addressing the sensory issues occurring in the feet of individuals with Asperger's. The most embarrassing aspect of sitting in a class circle begins when nearly immediately, your feet go numb or fall asleep. This happens quickly, consistently, and annoyingly. Especially when the instructor tells everyone to jump up and begin doing something physical involving leg movement. Having experienced this constantly for the last two years of attending the university, I was blown away to hear Christian Stewart-Ferrer whom himself has Asperger's, basically explain that if a bear crashed a room of full of people, the Asperger's individual would still be trying to wake their feet up while the rest of the people ran out of the room. Again, never would I have thought that this condition was applicable to anyone else.

Another dominant sensory issue (hyper or hypo) found in the autism community is the sense of smell. Personally, I have fared moderately well in this arena. I do detest perfume sections due to the variety of smells that overload my senses. The most specific smell that is eternally unbearable is the burning Palo Santo wood. I learned this while I was in the middle of class and one of the students (with permission) lit a piece and proceeded to ceremonially waft it around the classmates. It made me so nauseous I had to leave class. I have never reacted more strongly to any smell.

In congruence with auditory processing disorders, the sensitivity to sounds are a common theme in individuals with autism. I experience this most dramatically with the hypersensitivity to sudden loud noises. Eight years of serving in the military, especially in the field of explosives, might make this seem odd. Demolitions are timed and therefore predicted with great accuracies. The randomness of such a loud noise can be of no comparison.

I will never forget how ridiculed I was when I worked for General Mills®. Our job entailed producing corn and wheat squares for their snack mix line of products. The pellets used to form the squares were pneumatically pushed through pipelines under extreme pressure. Even in such a loud manufacturing environment, when a pipe coupling burst, it sounded like 20 shotguns fired in unison. I hit the floor prostrate in fear for my life. I was berated for quite some time. I imagine I appeared like a Don Knotts character known as Mr. Chicken.

I also have the misfortune of being able to hear nearly inaudible tones that I can only scientifically describe as some sort of resonance. It's hard to espouse on this, as I don't know often know the source from which it comes. Sometimes it is as simple as the whine

of a modem, computer, or other electronic device.

Special Interest Groups

Perhaps the greatest dichotomy of all Asperger's traits is found in the world of special interests. Special interests refer to the almost if not fully compulsive obsessive ideation on a specific subject matter. In my experience, this trait is as varied as the rest of them and it varies individually from subject matter to subject matter.

There is no lack of literature supporting testimonies of individuals that have deep profound interests (and knowledge) in things like trains, military aircraft, and the odd collectables. A great many of the subjects and interests last a lifetime for those individuals. I can't relate to those individuals as readily as I do to those who will read this and find likeness with their own nature.

My ability to obsessively hyper-focus on a subject seems to revolve around certain triggers. That's right, I get triggered. My triggers seem to revolve around three particular groups; love or passion, discrepancy (truth), and personal creativity.

The first and most easily recognizable form of special interest manifests as a creative project based on emotional infatuation with that mysterious creature of the opposite sex. Much like any other natural creature capable of 'gifting', I will do everything in my power to construct the most thoughtful and elaborate present for the woman I am vying to win. Unfortunately, when a very high functioning autistic person does that, the results can be overwhelming to the recipient. I tell myself that it is because society has all but aborted the art of courtship. I could be wrong. I'm normally not, but it has happened before. It is probably received as being simply too much. There is also the question of finding value in craftsmanship, which has obviously been overlooked due to the outlet mall society we live in. Either way, it doesn't stop me from doing it.

I once took a truly gigantic Mason® jar and created a rose-filled terrarium of sorts. Another time I made a tea candle lamp with what looked like stained glass windows, customized to her various hobbies. Another time, I took a panoramic photo and made one of those spinning lamps or nightlights, like the ones you see in stores that mirror an aquarium scene. These all sound simple, but I assure you they were not easily crafted.

I once took a Shrinky Dink® sheet of plastic to a concert venue and had the band Rising Appalachia (her favorite) autograph it. They had no idea what a Shrinky

Dink® was. These are full page pieces of plastic that you can color and draw on. You then place them in an oven for just a minute of two and they shrink down to a smaller, shinier, and thicker ornament, keychain tag, or whatever you're creating. Anyway, I made her an autographed plug in the wall mountain scene night lite. It was impressive, I must say. Then again, nobody does that type of stuff, so the value gets marginalized.

The most elaborate of gifts were created for a Christmas present. It was more like a Christmas adventure puzzle. I had two or three presents for her to open first. That left two more presents and a note. The recipient had to open the note and decipher it. It was written in white crayon, so you couldn't just read it, you needed to ink over it or soak it to make the writings visible. The note then told you to reference parts of each gift to figure out the combination to the first box. Once that step was performed, the box would be opened to reveal a small gift of a handmade wax letter seal stamp and some wax sticks [what she wanted]. In addition, there were two burlap-wrapped Sumerian inscribed clay tablets and another note. The note required you to use the Sumerian tablets to solve a medium-level equation, the answer revealing the combination to the last present. The last present was a miniature golden Ark of the Covenant which was filled with a matching pendant, earring, and ring set of her preferred stone. I left a whole lot out, but hopefully you get the idea. The bigger point is that this was an all-consuming obsession that I invested weeks if not months into creating.

The second special interest group falls into the classification that I call discrepancy. It is the autistic version of being a social justice warrior. I am not moved by societal issues, but I am absolutely compelled when it comes to uncovering the truth. When I talk about the proverbial switch getting flipped, this group reigns supreme. I am not aware of the moment it gets flipped, and in this category, there is no dimmer. It is 100% ON and will not switch to OFF until total and absolute resolution has been found. This is the most extreme subjects of hyper-focus.

The aforementioned pattern hiding behind perfect squares (and cubes for that matter), fall into this group. An obstacle or question is raised and just like that video of Newton, Einstein, and Darwin, I will stop at nothing to reach a solid conclusion. This was what led me to learning I that I have High Function Autism or Asperger's Syndrome. It led me from knowing absolutely nothing about electrons to being able to teach it to kids in just two days.

A couple of years ago I got pulled over by a State Patrol Officer and issued a ticket for speeding. I was doing 74mph in a 65mph zone. I was courteous and polite, but I was slightly perturbed at the whole concept. I had gotten one or two speeding tickets in the past, but I just paid them and went about my business.

For some reason, this time the whole concept seemed less than Constitutional. Curiosity combined with a sense of justice raised the question to a level requiring research, and I love research when there's an internal desire for truth.

The next thing I know, I am downloading and printing the Declaration of Independence (I figured I should start at the beginning), The Federalist Papers (I don't recommend printing this), The U.S. Constitution, and Bouvier's 1856 Law Dictionary. I was heading to the bookstore to buy the latest version of Black's Law Dictionary. I was reading multiple states' constitutions, and going to the local libraries to read the county and state codes, ordinances, and regulations. I was noting the companies involved with producing and managing Drivers Licenses, as well as the chain of command from revenue to transportation to patrol. I consumed anything I could find regarding traffic law. It then dawned on me that my small university has an agreement with one of the best law schools this side of the Mississippi. I was spending hours reading through the American Jurisprudence. It is incredibly true that ignorance is no excuse when it comes to the law. That refers to both the law and the rights of individuals. I do not offer legal advice. It is not my obligation to teach others the truths that sit dusty on the shelves of public libraries and law school bookshelves. This is the most I will say on any type of published platform, but what I learned was truly illuminating, and proved rewarding.

I should note here that many years ago I added ancestry and genealogy to my list of special interests. In a time when I'm hearing that a statue of George Washington just got torn down, I can tell you it is of utmost importance to know who you are to the best of your ability.

For example, my 6th Great Grandfather was Col. Richard Jones III. He served in the Virginia House of Burgesses (our earliest form of governance) for Amelia

County. His neighboring Colfax county House member was a close friend. His name was George. When the Declaration of Independence (written by Thomas Jefferson, also in the Virginia House of Burgesses) was announced, George, Thomas, and Richard were all immediately subject to death by hanging without trial. Col. Richard Jones III would later serve at rank of Colonel under now General George Washington's Army. Since his son, my 5th Great Grandfather served at the rank of Capt. at the same time, it made them one of only 6 father/son commissioned officers to serve.

It pays to know your history, to truly understand the legal function of the Preamble, and to master the definitions of words such as eponym and capitonym. I enjoyed being able to walk away from a special interest that has great usefulness in society.

A more controversial special interest I stumbled upon was solar physics. It started as an inquiry into the dynamics of the climate and a search for validating science that supports a narrative that has been distributed by the media, politicians, and celebrities. I would never have considered the sun controversial. Ironically, it is incredibly controversial. I am attempting to keep this entire body of work free from citations so I will not elaborate, but essentially, I have learned that global warming was not only a false narrative, but there are far worse issues to be worried about.

The truth is that what little warming was experienced has officially collapsed as we are plummeting towards a cooling period. The sun has a regular maximum and minimum phase that lasts around 11-11.5 years between high and low points of activity. A complete solar cycle will last roughly 22 -23 years. Beyond the immediate high and low cycles, there is a greater solar minimum and maximum phase that occurs roughly every 400 years. Unfortunately, we are heading fairly rapidly towards a Grand Solar Minimum. That is the colder of the two. This is and will affect every part of society, but is not a permanent change in climate. It will, however, be detrimental for the next several decades. The majority of this century will certainly suffer the impact.

I don't know how much I should divulge about this topic. It certainly will never get covered by mainstream media, but I do encourage the science-lovers of you to explore the works of physicist and professor PhD. Henrik Svensmark, Danish National Space Institute, Professor Emeritus PhD. William Happer, Princeton University, and plasma physicist PhD. Anthony Peratt, Los Alamos National Laboratory.

The most enjoyable and rewarding special interest was initiated while playing with a vape pen and a $1 laser pointer in the dark. In a flashing moment I realized that if you could control the flow of the atomized stream while merged with a broad beam laser in one single portable device, you could create what I coined a Light Synchronized Atomized Beam Illuminating Refractor, a Light S.A.B.I.R.

I had this revelation while taking a course on entrepreneurship and social innovation. I showed my University President and begin the U.S. patent application process. I tried to file it on May 4th, but it ended up being dated May 6th. I tried my best to pay homage. Oh well at least I had it on file. I put the paperwork in my safe and basically forgot about it. I figured the right idea or opportunity would arise naturally and was content knowing I simply had invented the sci-fi (non-lethal) weapon of my childhood.

In March of 2019, I realized I was approaching May. I was wondering how you could create a balance between generating a fair compensation for my idea, not risk getting manipulated by the major toy manufacturers, and allowing others to advance their own creation (and even market it) with an equally fair and minimal investment. Reflecting upon the teachings of my social innovation class, I decided I would do something I am not aware of anyone else ever doing before. I decided to publish my invention and included all of the diagrams along with construction advice in book form. By using this method, my idea and diagrams receive proper protection, but the idea itself becomes public use. I then began writing my first book.

On April 15th, I took 24 proof copies to the Chicago Star Wars™ Celebration. It was the first time I had ever gone to anything closely related to a cosplay event, but I had a blast! I was able to give a signed copy of my book to a personal hero, Professor Michio Kaku at a lecture he gave downtown the first night I was there. I was also able to get pictures with and give personalized copies to Forest Whitaker, Bobby Moynihan, Sam Witwer, Billy Dee Williams, John Ratzenberger, and Hayden Christensen. I handed the rest of the books out randomly to whenever I felt led.

Also, I gave copies to Darth Vader & Chewbacca, just because.

On May 25th, 2019, (5+25+2+0+1+9=42) at age 42, and on the 42nd Anniversary of my favorite sci-fi movie, the Return of the Jedi (Marquand, Richard, dir. *Star Wars Episode VI: Return of the Jedi.* Twentieth Century Fox, 1983. Film), I officially published The Greatest Toy Never Made: The Light S.A.B.I.R. Patent.

I was hyper-focused on perfecting the design and description until the patent application was filed.

I was hyper-focused throughout March to write a book, design a cover, get blurbs for the back, format the whole thing, learn copywrite info, file with the Library of Congress, verify the printed copy looks good, and take them on the road towards Chicago.

Upon returning home, I was hyper-focused on building a working protocol, and withing three days I had succeeded.

The last special interest group that will trigger my mind or flip that mental focusing switch revolves around personal creativity.

About 5 years ago I was learning about some non-western practices. I started researching chi-energy and other things I would stumble across. In my research I came across the practice of meditation. I read as many of the scientific studies I could find. I read all about the many benefits that were gained from a practice of meditation.

My next step was the practice, itself. I read and watched many sources on techniques, duration, frequency, and form. Basically, I took every single technique I could find, extrapolate the common denominators, and build one single style.

I then began implementing my practice. I started by using my phone and timing myself to see if I could go two minutes clearing my mind, acknowledging any thought that may arise, and then mentally pushing it aside. Two minutes led to five minutes, five turned to fifteen, and eventually working myself up to forty-five minutes. This whole time I retained the mentality that it was just game and never tried too hard or had no great expectations. I began meditating multiple times per day and eventually spend the breadth of a sunny day meditating. I did lose track of time, but it was around 8 hours. I found it easy to do. Incredibly easy. I have only later learned that I am not some "arrived Master". That numbness in my extremities so immediately experienced when sitting Indian-style or lotus position and the fact that I am able to hyper-focus without emotional thoughts running through my head, made the process almost natural. Again, thanks to ASD.

Another example hyper-focused during this timeframe, was on the subject of sungazing. I have mentioned it previously so I don't feel the need to elaborate, but the end result of me standing 45 minutes in shorts and a t-shirt while barefoot on snow felt like I had some ability due to mastery. There again, this experience and physical tolerance is actually a trait of those on the spectrum.

I love reading articles, science journal publications and anything else that adds to my knowledge base. I prefer to do that online or through media. I have never been a book reader. Reading books tend to put me to sleep. I don't know why. When living in Amarillo, I had no great means to entertain myself and decided to visit the local library. I checked out a great number of books on the subjects I thought would be interesting. I found that if I could juggle a large stack of various subjects, I could read an enormous number of books. The key was to have something else on hand to immediately switch to the second I grew uninterested.

I read books on thinking like Sherlock Holmes, physics made easy, Nietzsche's Beyond Good and Evil,

Ben Franklin's Autobiography, Medical Dictionaries, and Plato. I read everything from Don Miguel Ruiz to the LSAT Advanced studying manual. By the end of this hyper-focused reading stretch (that only lasted a month), I had read twenty-eight or so books. Again, this is from a guy who couldn't finish a book to save his life.

One special interest was when I decided to actually *write* a book. I went to one of the craft stores and found the nicest blank leather-bound book I could find. I bought a calligraphy set and spend days upon days handwriting a book that had chapters on personal quotes, meditation, sun gazing, the mathematical patterns, why π has no end, how the swastika was originally a representation of Ursa Major's 7 brightest stars and used by all civilizations to reference seasons, direction, and time as the night passes.

The list never ends. I dive into art, music, and anything else that sparks me until I have exhausted myself on it, then discard it as quick as I clung to it.

Unfortunately, typically any other aspect of my life is immediately sided, the level at which depends on the intensity of focus. That is the downside of extreme focusing.

COVID-19 & H.F.A.

The most recent special interest was something that has affected the whole planet in one way or another. When Covid-19 started making the smallest of headlines, I thought I would see what this whole thing was about. I actually wondered if this would become a subject I would eventually be consumed by, and it was.

It started by reading foreign articles and reports of the virus. It's nothing for me to see the patterns and I could immediately tell this was going to be widespread.

By mid-February I had begun using my web browser to translate the ongoing studies by Chinese medical doctors into English. I read every single possible study I could find. I took great note of what was being used, how much was being used, and how often the doses were administered. I began doing the same with the medical reports from other countries that were beginning to experience a rise in cases.

I immediately purchased gloves, hand sanitizer, goggles, and N-95 masks. I also began aggressively doubling my supplies or non-perishables. Again, this was in mid-February.

At that same time, I remembered once reading about how survivalists and prepper-types would acquire medicine marketed for animal use, but containing prescription ingredients. I knew that chloroquine phosphate was the most effective treatment being used for patients who had contracted SARS-CoV-2.

I immediately began to search and see if there were any sources of chloroquine phosphate available for purchase. It turns out, I could only find one single absolutely pure form of chloroquine phosphate without a prescription (or owning a laboratory). I was able to source the distributor to a company called New Life Spectrum® They sold only one specific product that was purely chloroquine phosphate. This product was called Ick Shield© powder. It was not a fish tank cleaner like many uninformed talking heads would chatter. It was for use in quarantine tanks only. I personally verified with the manufacturer that it was 99.99% pure. I had already estimated that it was, because the ingredients only listed one thing. It was listed by its International Union of Pure and Applied Chemistry (IUPAC) name. By using such a proper chemical nomenclature, it was incredibly easy to verify.

Once I had verification of chemical content and confirmation of purity, all I had to do was work out the physical dosage. The dosage calculation is as important as any other step, because when you are dealing with pure base form powder, you can cause great harm, even death. Let's say for example, a country is giving patients 500mg per dose. That dosage is in pill form. The pill *actually* contains only 300mg of the active ingredient. The other 200mg are binders. Hopefully you can see how exponentially dangerous that can become if you aren't meticulous about what you are doing. Chloroquine phosphate is and has always been incredibly safe at moderate dosages when taken for limited amounts of time. It has been used against everything from Ebola to rabies.

Now I was set! I knew what was coming, I had a small supply of PPEs, I had enough non-perishable goods for two people to sustain for maybe a couple months. I even had my own supply of chloroquine phosphate.

I began sharing with my friends on social media in great detail and with supporting scientific evidence (documentation) what I had discovered. I'm not a doctor and made no recommendations. I just established a fact-pattern for protecting myself during this newfangled pandemic. This also included known drug interactions and health variables that are incongruent with the chemical compound's efficacy.

After reaching resolution about being able to wisely protect myself using a concrete scientific approach, I wondered what the viral pattern of the SARS-CoV-2 was. I was able to find a couple of studies that had clear markers of patient symptom onset and disease progression. Using that data, I was able to extrapolate the cycle of viral load and verify congruency with death spikes. To make an elaborate story condense, I was able to pinpoint the viral cycle centered on a 6-day load cycle. The bulk of patients experiencing viral load became symptomatic after six days. Six days after becoming symptomatic, the largest spike in deaths occurred. Twelve days after becoming symptomatic, an even larger spike in deaths were seen. Fourteen days after becoming symptomatic, the death rate experienced its largest spike.

I have friends who have independently verified their personal symptomatic peaks occurring on day six and day twelve. I was able to use real-time data from the various COVID-19 monitoring websites, to accurately depict death-rate spikes in countries such as Italy. I made an elaborate post that I tried to share with every reputable medical or government source I could find. I firmly believe that many lives could have been saved if instead of maintaining a steady dose of prescribed medicine, the dose was temporarily increased on fifth day, thereby circumventing the viral load peak point.

In addition to raising awareness of the viral load cycle and personal acquisition of chloroquine phosphate, I also raised awareness of the use of hydroxychloroquine in combating SARS-CoV-2. I was addressing this issue long before the Coronavirus Taskforce brought it to public attention.

I did everything I could think of. I know of CDC employees, Grammy® Award winning artists, tons of friends, and personal family members that were able to prepare in advance and combat this virus accordingly. I am the reason Ick Shield® powder sold out completely online. It was also comforting knowing that people I knew that were on hydroxychloroquine for various reasons were able to secure their refills before there was an absolute run on the product. I even created a page called Science for Nurses that was specifically for educating the nursing and EMT community on science-based discoveries and information sharing.

Mr. Know It All

A sad and uncomfortable byproduct of a high functioning individual with autistic traits is that they are often never understood for what is actually driving them. Instead, they are met with resistance, ridicule, and as a form of neurotypical defense, name calling. Undoubtedly, if you have ever experienced being called a "Know it All" with any semblance of frequency, you might just be on the spectrum.

Very few people understand the overwhelming inability to simply let something go, or ignore the inaccuracies in another's comments. In as much as researching obsessively a particular topic may be, that same compulsion is manifest in the intolerance of misinformation, abhorrence of adulterated facts, or even the complete disregard for context.

It doesn't matter how long you have been friends with someone, apparently the bulk of society does not like to be corrected. I don't understand this at all. If you present me with factual information that can legitimately truncate whatever I believed to be truth, I will not only accept it, but be grateful that you have contributed to my knowledge base. I know what I know, I know that I don't know everything, and I know there is an entire world of topics I'm fairly ignorant about. Nothing should be more difficult than reaching that conclusion.

I have lost my fair share of friends over my inability to ignore that which is inaccurate, or more accurately because I didn't know how to soften my correction. I wish I could. I wish I could scroll right past things that are obviously agendized and maladapted to fit narratives and biases. I can't do it. I don't know everything. I haven't studied everything, but unlike the neurotypical's subject exploration, if I research something, it is generally an all-consuming endeavor that doesn't become quelled by mere surface-level gendering. On the same note, I'm quick to admit a lack of knowledge on a particular topic. It doesn't make me feel inferior. I'm ready to hear anything new that may be useful to my learning.

Between a loosely constructed bias, and a sense of feeling personally attacked (which it is NEVER the case), someone on the spectrum with this trait is bound to experience the wrath of the uninformed. It is inevitable. I wish it wasn't.

If you are resonating with this, you are probably aware that as soon as factual information is no longer accepted or being countered, the other party's default mode is to attack the actual person (ad hominem) and therefore distance the conversation from the original subject matter. Nearly all meaningful dialogue and discussion will be forgone for name-calling.

Best Friend?

Another uncomfortable truth when it comes to traits of the high functioning autistic community is the lack of a best friend. This has never been more painfully obvious than it has been in my own life. Best friend. I don't even know what that is. It isn't that I wouldn't love to have one. They sound cool.

I can only relay my own perceptions and experiences and can never accurately speak for any type of community, because individuals vary. Left to my own assumptions, I can think of several reasons this is such an unattainably lofty goal or desire. If you are naturally an introvert, you desire close lasting friendships, but don't know the protocols, you have an unfortunate compulsion to correct inaccuracies espoused by others, you naturally miss social cues, you seem to lack empathy, you're always talking about the same odd topics consisting of subjects that absolutely nobody else around you is interested in, your intelligence or subject matter delivery appears arrogant, you have compromised executive functioning skills so your life appears to be a haphazard pile of shambles, so exactly *who* would want to be your friend?

While I await your response, I'll begin writing another chapter.

Social Isolation

There are many factors that contribute to the social isolation of those individuals with high functioning autism. If you stack all the information accrued in the previous chapters, it makes sense why one would isolate. It is part preference, part avoidance, part acceptance.

I have never been truly happy in the normal realm of society for any length of time. I never had the desire to do those things society expects. Most things don't make sense to me, when it comes to humanity. The happiest I have ever been was when I gave up on everything. I worked long hours in a corn and wheat dust-filled environment where system engineers couldn't articulate the need to use trisodium phosphate in the batches of product being made for human consumption. They had no safety concerns for the inhalation of calcium carbonate, despite solid scientific evidence supporting the data. I made good money at the cost of actually living life. It sucked. I had an ex-wife that would manipulate her way out of court-ordered visitation with the only two sources of unconditional love I had ever known (outside of my own parents), there was no legal arm of enforcement, so I gave up. I concurred to her doctrine of laches and lived the life of a minimalist. I got rid of all the nice material possessions and lived off of a miniscule military disability. I slept in a tent or hammock and travelled from place to place living on granola bars and ramen noodles. I did my laundry in a 5-gallon bucket using creek water and a notched-out toilet plunger as an agitator. It was amazing. I still spend most of my time in total and complete isolation. Sometimes it was/is on National Forest, Army Corp, or BLM land. Even if I'm at home, I am still in near total isolation.

Multiple times I have been at home outside smoking a cigarette. when I see a neighbor that I actually like, pull up. I will quickly go back inside, just so I don't have to have an interaction of trivial discussion.

Is that normal? Well, to quote the legendary Nashville songwriter Travis Meadows, "God got it right when he made us all. The wires got crossed in a few. One man's strange is another man's normal, whatever normal means to you". Social isolation is normal to me.

Oddities

Each and every one of us know ourselves to some extent and should have enough sound mind to be honest with who we are. This continuing exploration of the craziness I call my life never ceases to reveal new truths. I spent 39 years not knowing if I was smart, average, or less than. I spent 43 years not knowing what Autism, Asperger's, or High Functioning Autism meant. I had a clue. What I didn't have was a clue that it would be anything I could relate to, let alone *completely* relate to. All I know is that I've always been weird. That's the story of my life.

I have no doubt there is a good probability of genetic inheritance to being on the spectrum. I grew up with a father that was OCD before we even knew what OCD was. We used to joke about it, but he was absolutely meticulous about things. It made sense though. He built custom cabinetry, and he was phenomenal at it. Ironically, later in life he joked as he told me he failed woodworking in high school, not once, but three times. His father was an engineer and worked for an astounding 40 years on the Elgin, Joliet and Eastern Railway in Chicago. My mother's father was an underwater welder for the Navy and was immediately assigned to Pearl Harbor after the attacks to assist in rebuilding it. He built his own small tractor, had a winchline running directly from the boat ramp to his boatshed (no vehicle needed), and built a metal boat dock that is still floating today, almost 50 years later.

He was Ted Turner's personal mechanic when Mr. Turner would partake in the yacht races in Savannah, GA.

I was all excited to take Sanskrit when I got to university. I was following along in class just like the masses. I had a great instructor. I was excited. Yeah, I mentioned that already. I'm making a point. Having a non-typical brain weighted towards pattern recognition is a blessing for independent exploration. It is an absolute curse when trying to learn subjects the neurotypical way.

I spent one night simply studying the "letters" of the Sanskrit alphabet, and noticing how they were constructed. In one flashing moment I realized what I was looking at. I was seeing the intent in the shapes. Sanskrit is famous for being very specific on how the sounds are made using the 5 mouth positions. What they don't tell you is that the Sanskrit symbols are actually morphed drawings of the actions of the mouth.

Even worse than missing the most obvious of ancient intents and quite helpful learning mechanisms, it was abundantly obvious that direction of the Sanskrit alphabet was (and is still) being taught in reverse. Imagine the arrogance of telling your teacher on week two of Sanskrit, "You're teaching it wrong!". But it was a truth I refused lay aside for the sake of class. I tried, but it was all I thought about during class. It is the equivalent of teaching math starting at 99 and working your way backwards, never being told that it is simply a binary rotation of 5 positions each. But that is a whole book unto itself. When I tried to explain that π can never have a single endpoint because man is attempting to use a binary language to describe a singularity that is neither, my own aunt suggested I "stay off the pot". That is what it is like being neurotypical.

I know I have oddities though. I'm not OCD like my dad, but an old girlfriend of mine noticed how I was compelled to straighten floor rugs and she used to mess them up ever so slightly and laugh from afar as she watched me straighten them. Ha-ha, Katie. You were probably the first to raise my awareness of having any kind obsessive compulsion.

Another odd compulsion I have is a classroom curse of sorts. Once I am properly seated in class, I immediately start counting the number of like objects in the classroom to see if I can count down from 10; 10 bulbs, 9 window panes, 8 electrical outlets, etc. Stupid, I know.

On a side note, writing this book has shown me that I type the word 'the' twice, seemingly without exception.

Body Language

Sometimes you find yourself down a rabbit hole that has a benefit you aren't immediately aware of. When I was in Amarillo, I yet again fell victim to a special interest. I don't remember what triggered or set off this obsession, but the topic was on reading body language.

Before I knew I it, I was at the public library and Amarillo College's library reading every single book I could find that addressed reading body language. I watched every single lecture (F.B.I. and otherwise), and I even binge-watched every single episode of Lie to Me. I didn't just watch it though, I studied the episodes, rewinding, pausing, evaluating every nugget of knowledge, and observing closely every micro expression.

I found it fascinating to learn this whole new language. I enjoy people watching from afar. Studying and observing are naturals for me, and this topic provides for so much insight. Watch their eyes. Are they recalling or are they creating? Do their shoulders rise when they respond? Do their yes' or no's operate in congruent nature with the direction their heads are moving? How are their breaths? Do they exhibit a micro twitch when forced with an uncomfortable question? Look at their body language. Her legs don't position towards interest in him. These are all some of the fun questions that can be posed while people watching, whether it is in person or on a televised congressional inquiry.

Here's a freebie for anyone on the spectrum. Apparently, people don't like to know that you can tell if they're lying by studying micro expressions, especially if it is someone you like. It is apparently not beneficial to disclose how many hundreds of hours you have spent studying this. Personally, it would make me question the integrity of someone who is uncomfortable hearing that, but whatever. I couldn't lie to save my life. My body language would look like a robot shorting out, ha-ha. I do enjoy using the science I have learned to evaluate those on tv news clips and internet videos. It is quite enlightening.

This is a useful curriculum, but it is much harder to execute when you are in dialogue with the person you are reading, because for me, everything is a distraction and there are plenty of clues and cues that I don't get during personal interactions, like sarcasm.

Sarcasm In-Person

This whole book is beginning to seem like just a long list of bad traits. That isn't my intent. It is however, an accurate reflection of my reality. One of the more common things that gets lost on me is sarcasm. Not all forms of sarcasm, just the mildest of forms and when delivered in person. I don't even know if this is worth mentioning, but in my world, it is frequent enough to include. I don't know why this is. I get Monty Python's sarcasm. My Dad raised us with high doses of humor. I can only assume that it is in part due to me trying to process everything else going on in the atmosphere of the conversation, or it may be due to the delivery of the comment. Either way, there is a fair chance that I may be completely oblivious to the use of sarcasm.

Test Yourself

With everything I had learned, I began wondering what type of tests there were online that may help gauge the accuracy of my newly arrived conclusion. There are many helpful sites that I encourage anyone who may be coming to a similar realization to explore. Pyscholgy-tools.com has several tests you can take. They have an Empathy Quotient test as well as an Autism Spectrum Quotient test. I would recommend taking both of them to better formulate any type of conclusion. Psychcentral.net offers a short Autism Screening Quiz you can take. I will ashamedly share my results of each below.

Short Autism Screening Quiz

You scored a total of **34**

Autism

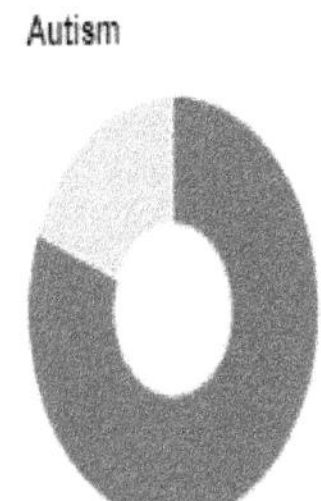

Autism Likely

Based upon your responses to this autism screening measure, you have symptoms associated with an autism spectrum disorder diagnosis. People who've scored similarly to you on this screening measure will usually meet the diagnostic criteria for autism or Asperger syndrome, a milder form of autism.

People with an autism spectrum disorder often suffer from severe and sustained impairment in social interaction and the development of restricted, repetitive patterns of behavior, interests, and activities. The disturbance must cause clinically significant impairment in social, occupational, or other important areas of functioning.

You should not take this as a diagnosis of any sort, or a recommendation for treatment. However, some people with similar scores seek out further information and potential diagnosis & treatment from a trained mental health professional.

SCORING

	Then symptoms of...
31 & up	Autism likely
14 - 30	Autism possible
0 - 13	No autism symptoms

This is not a diagnostic tool.

Please consult a mental health professional for an actual diagnostic assessment.

Your score was 41 out of a possible 50.

Scores in the 33-50 range indicate significant Autistic traits (Autism).

Concerned about your score?

Chat online with a licensed therapist.

Your score was 7 out of a possible 80.

Scores of 30 or less indicate a lack of empathy common in people with Autism or Asperger's Syndrome.

Higher scores indicate greater levels of empathy.

Concerned about your score?

Chat online with a _licensed therapist._

It Never Ends

Life is always throwing new twists and turns my way, and I have learned to embrace them all. I am no good at establishing my own structure for living or functioning normally. I don't think I could optimize my talents or gifts in such a structured regiment. Part of me wouldn't wish this strange higher functioning version of autism on anyone. Another part of me realizes that if we all were like this; politicians would have a much harder time securing (and keeping) our votes because their emotional tactics would not work. More misinformation would get highlighted. Teachers would be educating students by explaining the patterns governing certain subjects and rely far less on subject memorization and regurgitation. That would increase understanding of the subjects being taught.

Society today has (for the most part) become so emotionally biased towards their own polarizations that logic seems to have no part nor value in discussion. Science is used out of context to promote agendas. Opposing viewpoints are not only written off, they are often attacked as being racist, sexist, or whatever else can be used to properly shame someone. History is not only lost, it is twisted to promote narratives, or even worse, disregarded completely.

I don't know how to successfully live in this world and fit in as if the people and things around me make sense. They don't. If I correct the information someone shares, they tend to feel it is *ad hominem* without even trying to process or verify what I am saying. If I try to share solid science with an individual, they refuse to read it, so I stay away from it all.

The benefit of my total disregard for bowing to the normalcy of this crazy world is that I can dive head first into something like electrons and within two days correct the predicted electron orbital configuration of and element that hasn't even been smashed into existence yet. Left alone, I can obsessively construct on paper and eventually in the physical a toy that was more fictional than the hoverboard. I can explore the topics that interest me, such as the "religion" of Mithraism and see it for what it was. I can easily see what knowledge they were trying to keep active and how their very practice was a useful preparation for what they were aware of.

It doesn't matter, if in general, no one understands me. What matters is that after 43 years, I am at peace knowing that finally,... I know me.

Thank You

for spending your time

and money to purchase and

read this.

If even one person is able to realize the source of their awkwardness and accurately attribute it to this odd disorder, it was all worth it.

Sincerely,

J. Matthew Jacobson

Referenced Work

The Spherical Nature of the Universe and the Laws that Facilitate Structure

This paper serves to identify in theory, the characteristics that shape and influence Universal containment.

It is my hope and intent to simplify this mysterious nature using the most rudimentary explanation possible for the betterment of all comprehension. New laws have been formulated to serve as the foundation of this theory.

J. Matthew Jacobson

Laws of Closed System Balance

1) A body's accumulation of mass must be directly proportional to the environment's degradation

2) Balance of a closed system must contain an outside force to facilitate movement

3) If the ratio of mass accumulation to degradation continually becomes disproportionate, the system will eventually settle into a steady state

Laws of Natural Spherics

1) A body's expansion, staticization, and compression will naturally seek maintenance of a spherical shape

2) Any deviation of this shape is the result of influence from an outside force

The Universe exists as a closed spherical system. Every electron, atom, and planet will naturally seek to obtain and maintain this form. This shape uniformly exerts and tolerates an optimal amount of force at the most perfectly attainable level of distribution. The containment found in a spherical system fosters cyclical continuity. The force that is responsible in the observable forms of pressure and resistance on celestial bodies would not be possible in an open system. Our Universe may not be the only universe in existence, but it is definitely a system unto itself.

The energy (most logically occurring in plasma form) is speculatively the most abundant matter in our Universe. It applies pressure to celestial bodies in much the same way a ball submerged in water would experience pressure. The pressure this dark or unmeasured plasma exerts on bodies may provide the answer to the question that has eluded humanity for centuries. What is gravity? I suggest it is simply the effects of a closed system pressure in the form of a relatively weak force. It is however, strong enough to pressure gases into an atmosphere.

The force dark plasma exerts decreases exponentially as the distance from the affected surface area increases, however, it is still present. This exponential diminution of force explains the question of how a galaxy can grow at increasing speeds as it propagates from the center. As the core force known as gravity diminishes, the pressure or resistance from dark plasma still exists keeping the galaxy (in this example) from instantly flying apart.

At great distances from the surface area of which dark plasma is applying force, there will continue to exist a quantifiable effect. This tight system will create an almost spider-webbed effect throughout the Universe. This force may have previously been partially or completely explained as belonging to gravity, but is in fact dark plasma fighting to reclaim the occupied space. It will still carry its desire to coalesce any celestial matter it comes in contact with, but may lack the energy to succeed. Understanding this concept will successfully transcend the dimensionally-lacking image of a bowling ball on a trampoline where another object rolls towards it. A more accurate and reliable image would be that of an ocean of dark plasma tightly surrounding objects in a tightly closed sphere. Celestial matter is constantly being met with pressure and resistance, but only with enough force to gradually shape and slow it. This force is every bit as equal in nature to the fixture and shaping of galaxies, planets, and atmospheres as the force which is attributed to the nomenclature referred to as gravity. It may very well be responsible for far more than currently believed or accepted in traditional and modern physics.

This dark plasma is electrically conductive. I speculate that deeper studies into this realm may produce incredible discoveries and huge breakthroughs as to a more detailed nature of this elusive matter and the dynamics of an electric universe. I dare to imply that the darkest areas of our Universe may be the result of an abundant amount of electric coalescence of this dark plasma.

Black holes prevent the Universe from entering into a closed system steady state. They are the universal tides that assist this weak plasmid sea of space. Without the vacuum provided and the space for movement it creates via displacement, motion would be hindered. The consumption and degradation resulting from black hole function augments all celestial movement.

As energy travels through the expanse of space incrementally slowing in speed, a hypothesis can be reached for the speed of energy slowing to a point at which it becomes a mass. This transition occurs at the outer-most reaches of the Universe.

The resulting creation may form a shell or membrane of sorts that serves to contain a Universe spherical in shape. A bound Universe prevents the immediate over-expansion that would be our immediate destruction.

Figures 1-3 from the book

The Greatest Toy

Never Made

The Light S.A.B.I.R. Patent

J. Matthew Jacobson
J. Matthew Jacobson is an 8 year veteran of the United States Air Force. He held a security clearance as a Munitions Systems Technician and was instrumental in launching the Shock and Awe Air Campaign. He is now a Peace Studies Major. He is a member of Mensa, the world's oldest High I.Q. Society.
Now the public can gain access to the technology that allows for the build of a 3D non-lethal ascending/descending daylight visible beam of light!
"A roadmap to democratizing the journey from the individual bubbling up of the creative process to fruits of that inspiration. Now we don't need permission to play with someone else's toys. Rather in this small volume we learn the lesson of ultimate sharing."
-Charles G. Lief, President, Naropa University
"Genius! He single-handedly introduced an unprecedented approach to market innovative ideas. He always showed a special level of potential and now his efforts will change the toy industry."
- Roby Johnson, Chief Master Sergeant, USAF
The Greatest Toy Never Made
The Light S.A.B.I.R. Patent

The following images ©2019

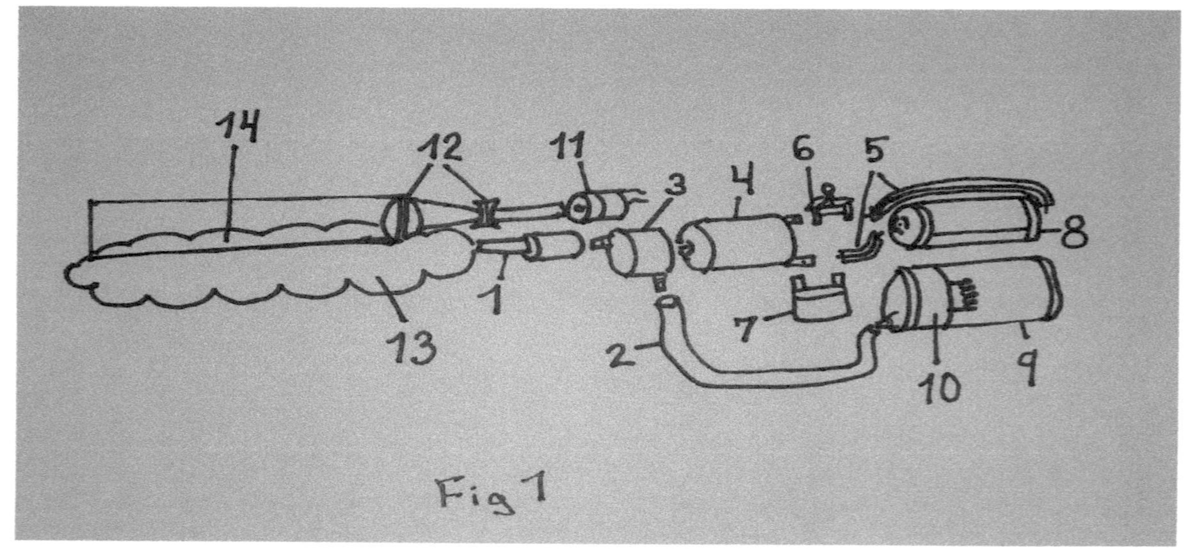

Fig 1

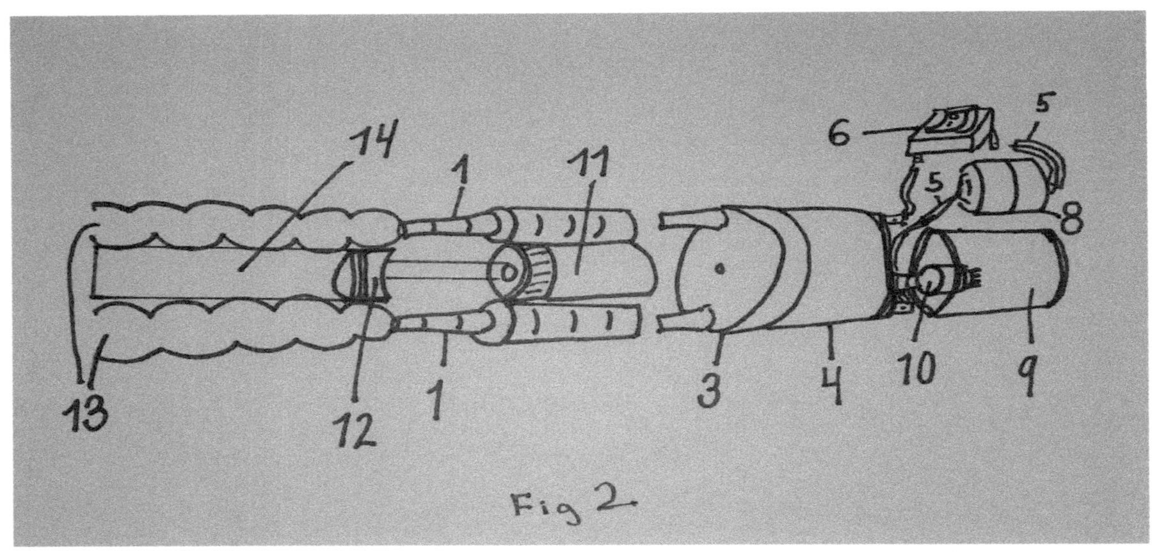

139

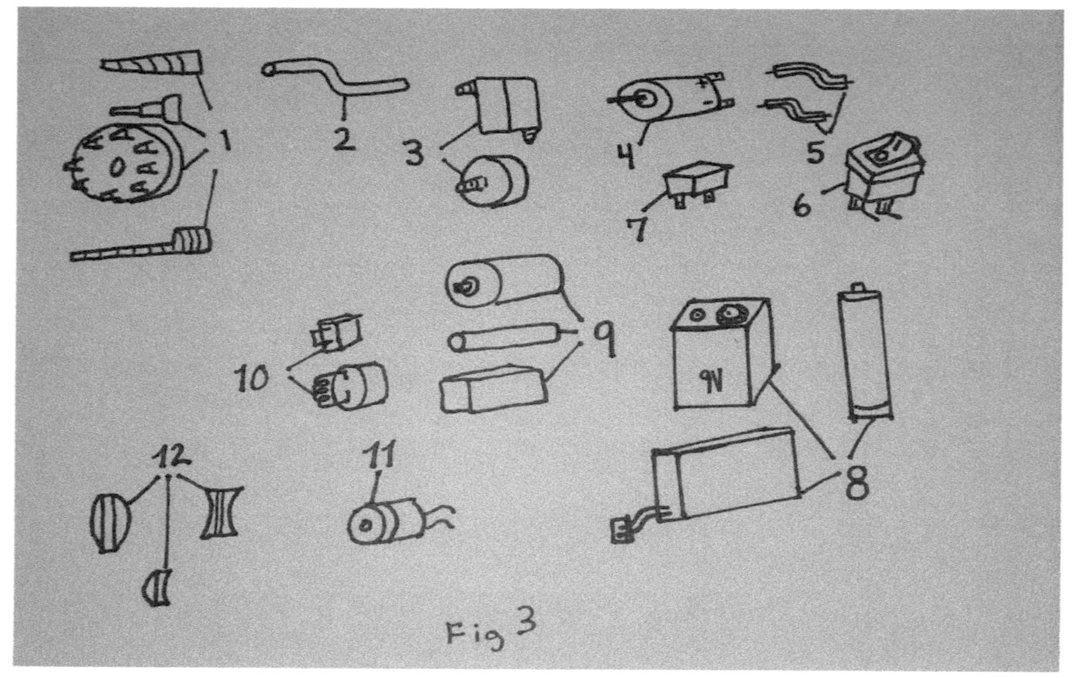

1
2
3
4
5
6
7
8
9
10
11
12
Fig 3

www.ingramcontent.com/pod-product-compliance
Lightning Source LLC
Chambersburg PA
CBHW040146160726
48006CB00014B/1638